MY FIRST REFERENCE LIBRARY

POWER

by Julie Brown and Robert Brown
Adapted from Steven Seidenberg's
Fuel and Energy

❧ BELITHA PRESS

Acknowledgements

Photographic credits:

Biofoto 57 bottom
Bodleian Library 27 top
British Coal 33 bottom
Edinburgh Photo Library 37
EWA 4
Geoscience Features 25
Susan Griggs/Sepp Seitz 5 left
Robert Harding Picture Library 17, 38, 46
Hutchison Library 5 top and bottom right, 6, 11
   bottom, 16, 19 right, 23 bottom, 27 bottom, 51, 59
   left
Japan Ship Centre 23 top
Kuvapörssi Oy 9 top
Frank Lane Picture Agency 39, 53
Magnum 8, 9, 13 bottom, 41, 44, 57 top
S & O Mathews 11 top
Christine Osborne 10
Science Museum Library 7 top
Science Photo Library 7 bottom, 33 top, 58
Robert Snedden 49
Spectrum 13 top, 19 left
Frank Spooner © Novosti 50
Charles Tait 21
A. C. Waltham 15, 35, 59 right
Zefa 28, 30

Illustrated by: Ross Watton

Series editors: Neil Champion and Mark Sachner
Educational consultant: Dr Alistair Ross
Editors: Robert Snedden and Rita Reitci
Designed by: Groom and Pickerill
Picture research: Ann Usborne

Contents

Words found in **bold** are explained
in the glossary on page 60

Energy

CHAPTER ONE

FUEL AND ENERGY

Energy exists in many forms. The most important kinds of energy are heat, light, electrical, **mechanical**, **chemical** and **atomic**. All forms of energy can be used to do work. When petrol is burned in a car engine its chemical energy makes the car run. Televisions and microwaves use electrical energy.

In this kitchen the lights, oven and microwave use electricity. The cooker uses gas. ▼

◄ In this factory, sparks fly as **robot** welders put a car together. Huge amounts of energy are needed.

▲ This power station in Hong Kong makes electricity. Power stations can use either coal, oil or nuclear fuel.

Stored Energy

Materials that store energy are called fuels. Many different kinds of fuels are used to produce heat and provide power for people's homes and for **transportation**. Food is the kind of fuel our bodies use. Like coal and oil, food is a store of chemical energy. Fuels can be solids, liquids or gases. Solid fuels include wood (chapter 2) and coal (chapter 6). The most important of the liquid fuels are made from oil (chapter 7). Gas is the third form fuel can take. Natural gas is found beneath the Earth's surface.

▲ Petrol and diesel are made from oil. Most cars use petrol. Trucks and buses use diesel.

5

A Short History of Fuels

Horses provide the power ▶ to plough this field. Animals are still an important source of power in much of the world.

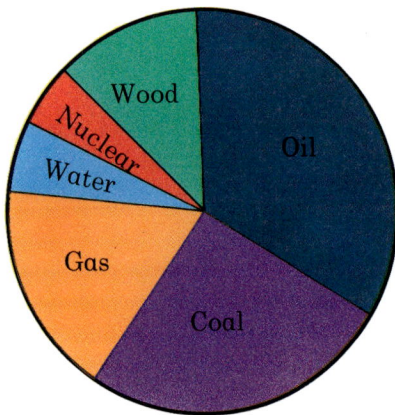

▲ This piechart shows the amount of energy the world gets from each type of fuel.

For thousands of years the muscles of people and animals were the only source of power. People used fire to provide heat and light but not to do work. Probably the first fuel used was wood. Later, people began to use the power of wind and water.

Fossil fuels

In the 1700s coal became the most important source of energy in Europe. By the end of the 1800s oil and gas began to take its place. These are all called **fossil** fuels. They are useful because they all contain large amounts of energy. They are also easy to move from place to place and store.

Nuclear power

Many people hoped that nuclear fuel would replace fossil fuels. Today we are not so sure, since nuclear power can be very dangerous. Our demand for energy keeps growing, however.

▲ Three hundred years ago huge **blast furnaces** were powered by coal.

▲ **Hero** invented this wood-powered steam-engine almost 2,000 years ago.

◀ A nuclear power station in Cumbria, England.

CHAPTER TWO
WOOD

The First Fuel

This piechart shows the amount of energy provided by wood compared with other fuels. ▼

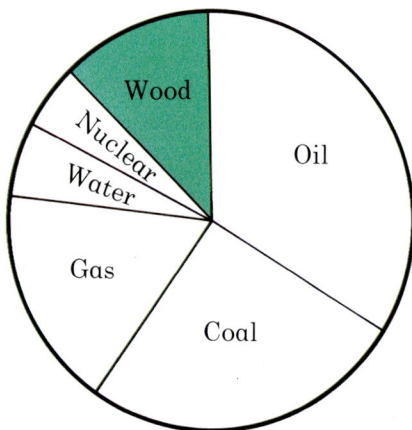

People in Mali, Africa, ▶ have to walk many miles to gather wood for fuel.

People learned to use wood as a fuel many thousands of years ago. They were able to stay warm and cook by building fires. Today wood is still an important fuel. In many poor countries wood remains the most important

source of energy. Wood provides more than half of Africa's energy supply. Wood is still used all over the world as a fuel.

An ideal fuel
In some ways, wood is an ideal

8

fuel. It is cheap and, unlike coal and oil, wood can be found almost everywhere people live. Wood burns easily without special equipment having to be used. Most importantly, wood is a fuel that should never run out. If people plant new trees to replace the trees that have been burned, this energy **resource** can be renewed. Fuels that can be replaced are called renewable energy resources.

▲ This factory in Finland produces wood pulp for paper-making. All the energy it needs comes from burning waste wood.

◄ Young trees growing on a **plantation** in Niger, Africa. These trees will replace others that have been used for fuel.

9

Charcoal

Although wood is a useful fuel, it is not always ideal. In some parts of the world it is not easy to find. People may have to spend much of their day searching for enough wood to cook their meals and keep them warm. Wood is also heavy to carry. Another problem with wood is that it does not burn very hot. It is hot enough for heating and cooking, but not hot enough for most industrial uses.

▲ Women in Orissa, India, walk many miles searching for and collecting firewood to heat their homes and cook their food. Charcoal is much less bulky than wood and provides more heat.

The world's first superfuel

Only about half of wood actually burns. Much of the weight of wood is made up of water. Charcoal is almost all carbon, which can burn. Charcoal is made by burning wood in special ovens

that keep the air out. This removes moisture and other **impurities** from the wood. Charcoal is much lighter than wood and burns much hotter so it can be used for more purposes.

▲ Wood is turned into charcoal in these ovens in East Sussex, England.

◄ A bread oven in Peru. By burning charcoal in the oven this man uses less fuel than if he used wood.

11

CHAPTER THREE

WATER

Water Power

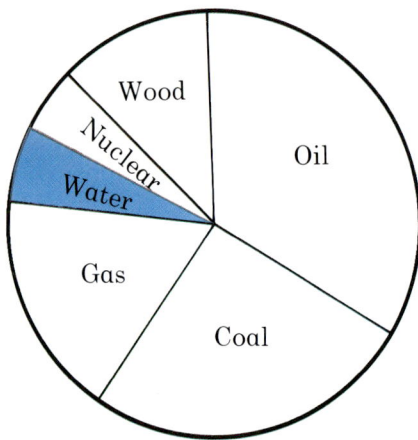

▲ This piechart shows that water is an important source of energy.

Water falls on the blades of this vertical water wheel (opposite). This turns the wheel, which rotates the central shaft. This can power simple machines. ▶▶

Horizontal water wheels use the force of flowing water to make the blades spin. ▶

Water wheels
The windmill and the water wheel are two of the oldest sources of power used by people. For more than 2,000 years water wheels have been used to power simple machines. Today water wheels are used to make electricity.

Two kinds of water wheel
There are two kinds of water wheel: horizontal and vertical. Vertical water wheels stand straight up out of a river or stream. Horizontal water wheels are put on their side in a stream.

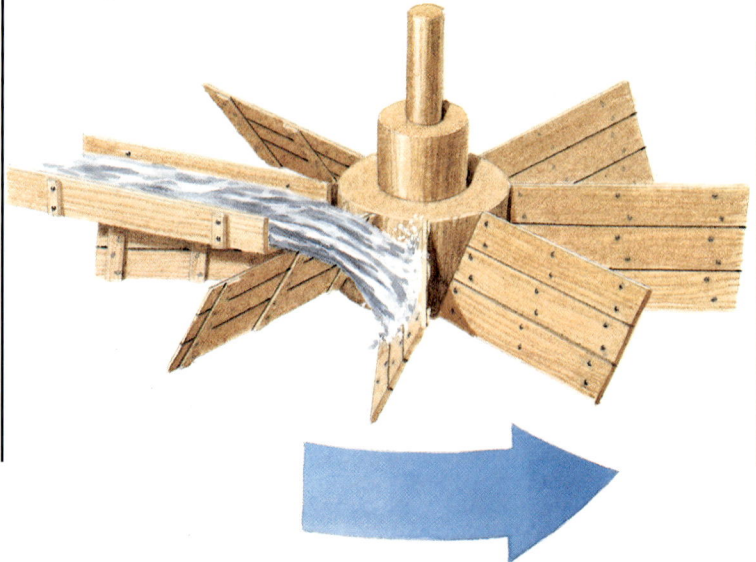

◀ A flour mill on the Isle of Skye, Scotland. Water falls from the chute above this vertical water wheel.

Water wheel wonders

● In 1086 there were 5,600 water wheels in England. This means that there was one water wheel for every fifty families living in England at that time.

● The biggest water wheel in the world is the Mohammadieh Noria water wheel (shown below) at Hamah, Syria. It is 2,000 years old and is as tall as a thirteen-storey building.

There were horizontal water wheels before there were vertical water wheels. They both work by turning the energy of flowing water into a spinning movement. This movement is then used to power simple machines such as grain mills, saws and grindstones. Horizontal water wheels produce less power than vertical ones.

▲ The world's oldest working water wheel in Hamah, Syria.

13

Hydro-electricity

Hydroelectric facts

● The USA and the USSR are the two countries that produce the most hydroelectricity.

● Hydroelectricity saves valuable fossil fuels. Hydroelectric power plants produce a massive amount of power. To get this electricity from oil we would have to burn an extra 4.3 billion gallons of oil every year.

Water collects behind this dam. Gates in the dam are opened, letting the water rush through a tunnel (see illustration opposite). This water is used to turn a generator that makes electricity. ▶

In the past, water wheels were used to power simple machines. Today water power is used differently. Dams are used to hold back water before it is let loose to turn **turbines**. These turbines then spin **generators**, which make electricity. Power made in this way is called hydroelectricity.

Clean and plentiful power

Hydroelectricity is a good source of power. It produces power without anything having to be burned. This means that it is a clean source of energy. It does not cause pollution like burning fossil fuels does.

Hydroelectricity is also a renewable resource. We will

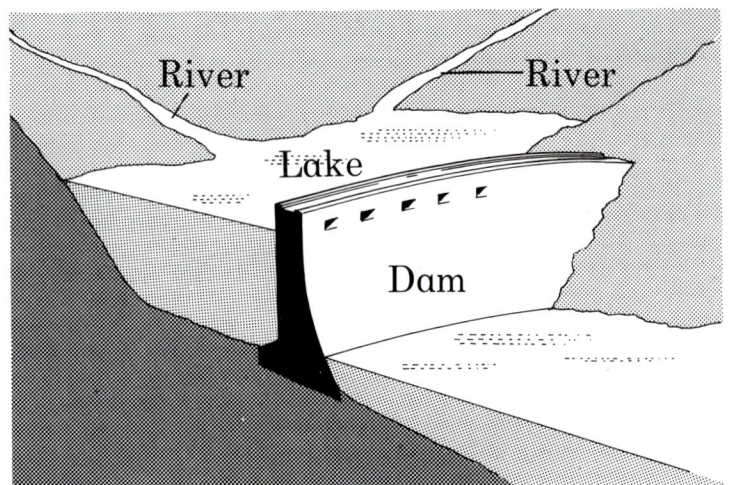

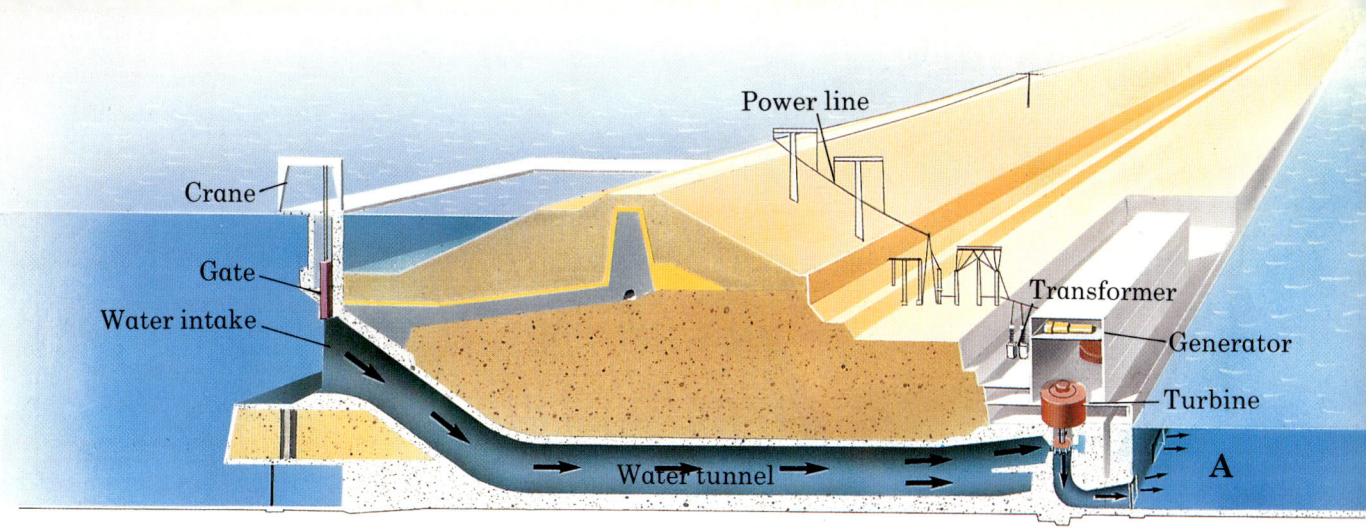

Crane

Gate

Water intake

Power line

Transformer

Generator

Turbine

Water tunnel

A

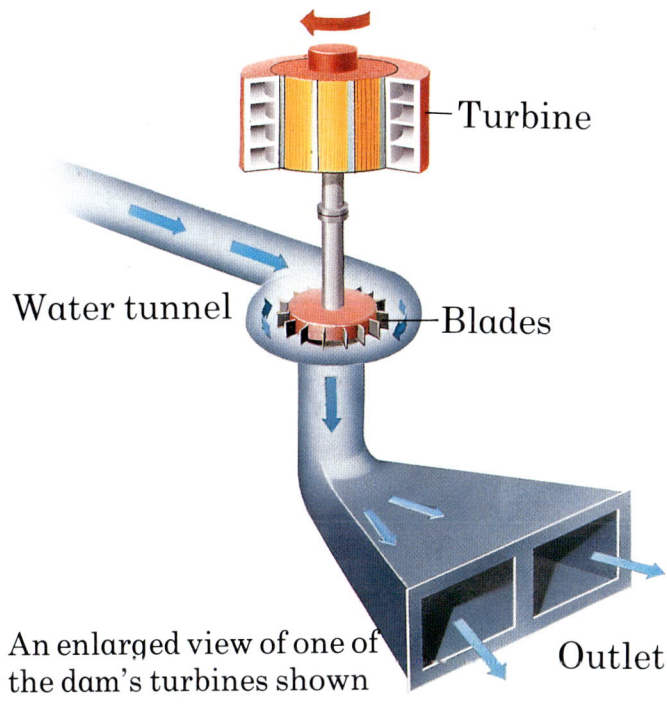

Turbine

Water tunnel

Blades

Outlet

An enlarged view of one of the dam's turbines shown at **A** above.

never run out of water. We will eventually run out of fossil fuels. The biggest producers of hydroelectric power are the USA, the USSR and Canada. Many countries do not have the water resources needed to generate hydroelectric power. It meets less than one-tenth of the world's energy needs.

▲ The Glen Canyon Dam goes across the Colorado River in Arizona, USA. Dams like this are huge. They can be hundreds of metres high.

The Future of Water Power

Water is plentiful, renewable and a clean source of energy. It has other advantages as well. The water stored behind dams to generate electricity can be used for other purposes. Lakes and reservoirs created by dams can be used for swimming, sailing and fishing. Dams can also provide water for farms and industries.

Tidal and wave power

Hydroelectric power stations need a regular supply of water.

Building a dam can ▲ flood the land. These trees were killed by rising water in the reservoirs behind the Tocantins River dam in Brazil, South America.

Dams help to ensure this but they often have harmful effects. Dams can flood valuable land. They can also prevent fish from swimming upstream to the shallow waters

where they breed. Scientists are looking for new ways to get energy from water that would avoid such problems. Recently they have been trying new ways to generate power from ocean waves and tides.

▲ An ocean barrage in Brittany, France, generates hydroelectric power from ocean waves and tides.

Tidal barrage

At St Malo, France, electricity is being produced by using the power of the tides. At high tide water is allowed to flow freely into the Rance River **estuary**. Before it is allowed to flow out again it is trapped by a kind of dam called a tidal barrage. The trapped water is let out by making it flow across turbines, generating electricity.

◄ In this experiment the power of the waves is being used to generate electricity.

CHAPTER FOUR

WIND

Power from the Wind

Wind produces a large amount of energy when it blows. If a way could be found to use the power of the wind efficiently all of our energy needs could be met. Part of the problem is that wind is not reliable. Sometimes there is not even a breeze.

The unseen force

From the earliest times people have been aware of the power of the wind. For thousands of years people have raised sails on their boats to catch the wind. When the wind blows, the boat is carried along. Some people have tried

Ships today use powerful engines to help them cross the sea. In earlier times large ships such as this one used wind power. These ships were called clippers. ▼

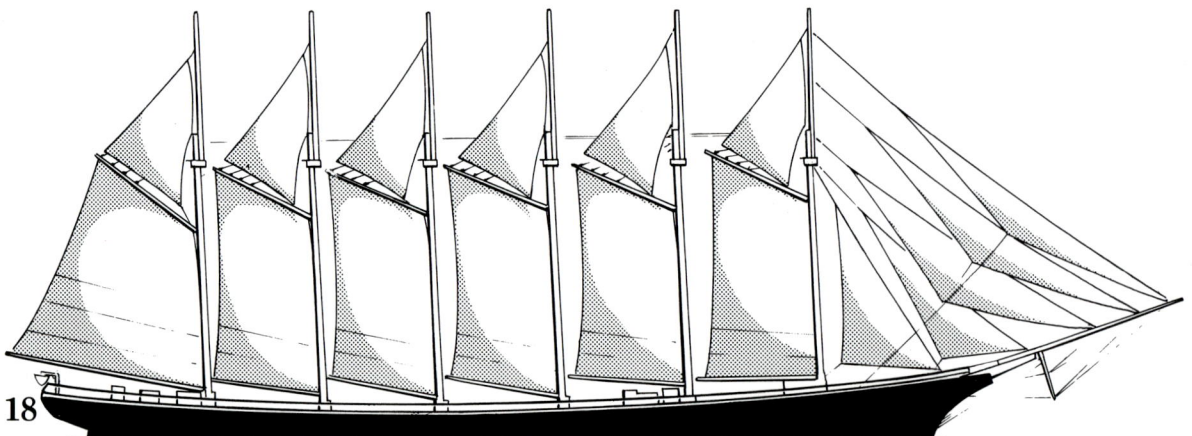

◄ These windmills are pumping water from a canal. They are a common sight in Holland.

▲ This windmill pumps water from under the ground for cattle to drink.

putting sails on wagons and carts but without much success.

Thirteen hundred years ago people in Persia (called Iran today) used windmills to power simple machines. At other times people have used windmills to grind grain (such as wheat and barley), saw wood, make paper or mix paint. After the steam-engine was invented, however, windmills were used less and less. Today windmills are used in many places to generate electricity. Many people are working to find better ways to use this clean, renewable source of energy.

Wind-pumps

There are many windmills in Holland. Perhaps they should be called wind-pumps. They are used to drain water from the land. The wind turns the sails. This turns the shaft, which is connected to a wheel with scoops all round it. The scoops lift the water into **canals** that carry it out to sea.

Windmills

This cross-section shows how a tower mill works. The fantail is used to steer the sails into the wind. The sails turn gears that turn millstones that grind grain. ▶

This tall wind turbine ▶▶ (opposite page) uses wind power to make electricity.

Mighty mills

Tower mills can be large. The tallest mill in Europe is in Holland. It is 33 metres tall, as high as a ten-storey building.

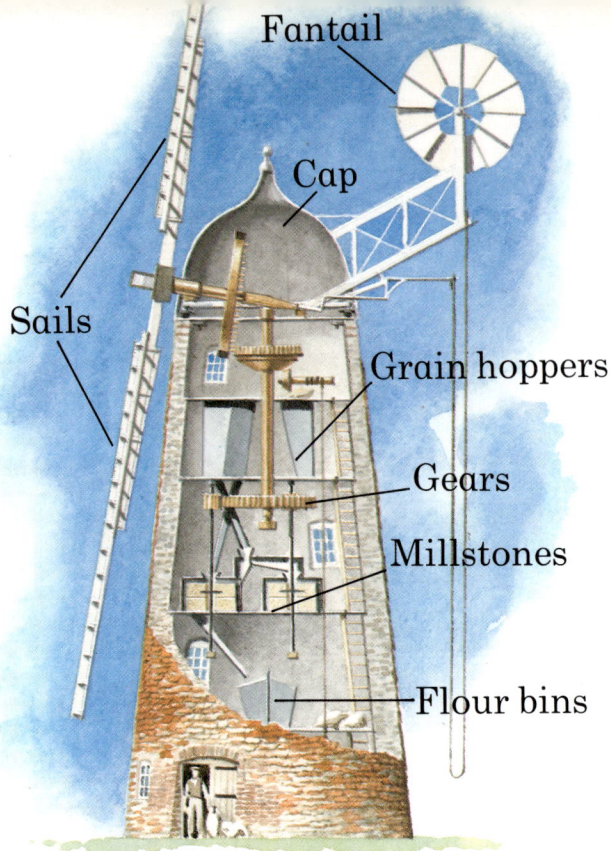

Fantail

Cap

Sails

Grain hoppers

Gears

Millstones

Flour bins

Early European windmills were called post mills because the box-shaped building sat on a central post. This allowed people to turn the windmill to face into the wind. Later windmill buildings were bigger and heavier and could not be turned. A movable cap on top was turned to face the wind instead of the whole building being moved. These were called cap mills or tower mills. They could produce more power than the earlier smaller windmills.

Sails

Early windmills had sails made of cloth, just like the sails on ships. Even today, some Mediterranean countries still use windmills with small triangular sails made of cloth. They might have as many as twelve of these sails. Later windmills had large wooden sails. Today's windmills often have just two sleek metal blades that look like aeroplane propellors.

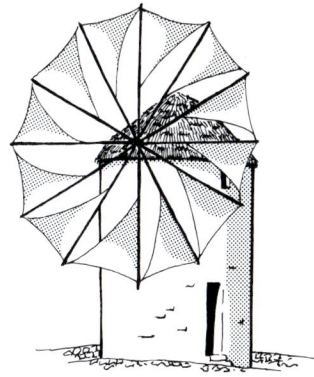

Top: Windmills with cloth sails are still found in Mediterranean countries.

Middle: A post-mill that can turn to face the wind.

Bottom: Mills like this are used to pump water on farms.

New Sources of Wind Power

A cross-section of a wind turbine. This machine turns the motion of the blades spinning in the wind into electricity. ▼

Windmills cannot work when there is no wind blowing. Another problem with windmills is that they take up a lot of space for the amount of energy that they produce. Over the years windmills have been replaced by more reliable sources of energy. On many farms, particularly in North America and Australia, windmills are still used to pump water for crops and animals.

The future of wind power

People are always searching for new ways to use wind power. New machines have been invented that use wind power more efficiently than the windmills of the past. These machines have turbines that turn the power of

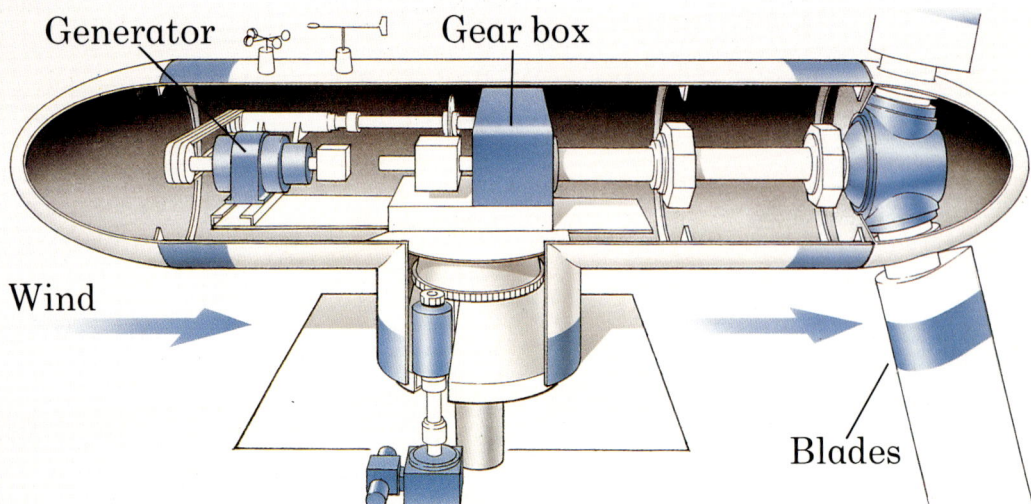

Generator

Gear box

Wind

Blades

the wind into electricity. Ways of storing this electricity need to be found so that it can be saved for use on calm days.

Some ships are now using a type of metal sail that can be turned into the wind.

▲ This large Japanese ship has large metal sails as well as engines.

These wind-powered electricity generators in California, USA, look like ◄ giant egg-beaters.

CHAPTER FIVE

FOSSIL FUELS

Fuels from the Past

Fossil fuels were formed from the remains of plants and animals that lived and died many millions of years ago. ▼

Coal, oil and gas are called fossil fuels. They are made of the remains of plants and animals that lived on the Earth a long time ago. Coal was formed from the remains of plants that grew in swampy forests. Over many years as the plants died, layer upon layer of them sank down into the swamps. The bottom layers were

Coal-mine

Oil rig

Gas well

turned into rock by the weight of the layers above. In this way, the plants were turned into coal.

Oil and gas were made in a similar way. The remains of tiny plants and animals in the oceans sank down to the bottom when they died. The bottom layers were turned into oil by the squeezing of the layers on top.

Using fossil fuels

When fuels such as wood or coal are burned a lot of heat is released. One of the earliest inventions to make use of this heat energy was the steam-engine. Later machines burned oil and gas for fuel.

▲ Fossil fuels are mostly found under the ground. Machines are needed to reach them.

This plant has been fossilized in coal. ▼

CHAPTER SIX

COAL

Black Diamonds

Coal has been used longer than the other fossil fuels. Coal provides a quarter of our energy needs today. ▼

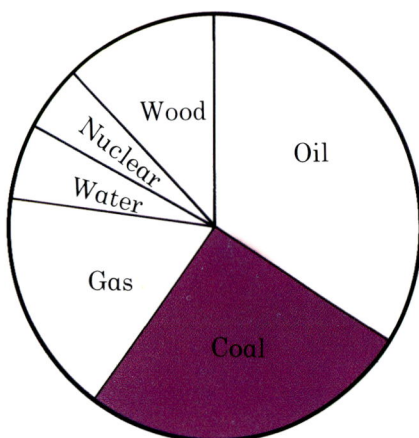

Coal is found on every continent. There are still huge amounts of coal in North America, Europe and Asia. ▶

All coal is mostly made of carbon. Sometimes people refer to coal as 'black diamonds', because diamonds are also made of carbon. Coal is valuable because it is a very important fuel.

Coal power

We don't know who first discovered that coal could be burned. We do know that about 4,000 years ago the people of Wales used coal to burn dead bodies. Around 2,000 years ago the Greeks and Romans used coal. Seven hundred years ago the great explorer Marco Polo

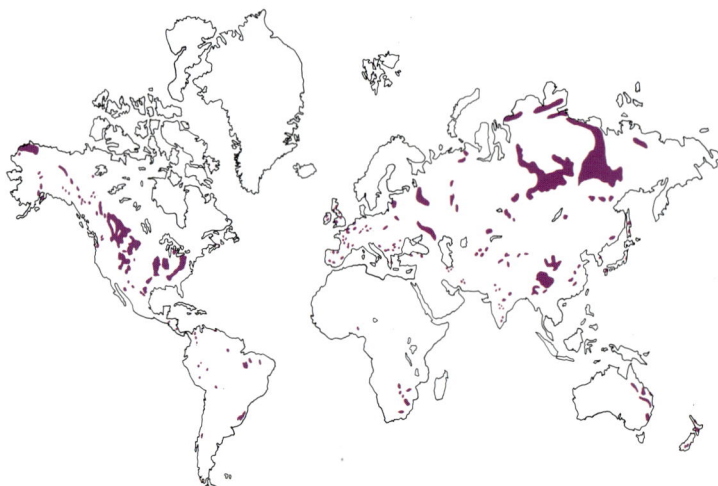

This illustration shows Marco Polo setting out on his travels from Venice to China 700 years ago. Among other things, he reported the use of coal in ◀ China.

brought back stories of people using coal in China. During the **Industrial Revolution**, coal became even more important as it was used to provide the power for the new machines that were invented then. Today, coal is mined mostly in the USSR, the USA, China and Australia. It is used in many countries.

Peat is like incompletely made coal. It can be cut up and dried for burning as fuel. ▼

Different Coals

This factory in Germany is burning lignite coal. A lot of pollution is sent into the sky. ▼

Lignite

Some coal is found in layers close to the Earth's surface. Other coal deposits are buried deep beneath the ground. Lignite coal is found near the Earth's surface. Because it is just under the ground it is easy to mine. It is brown and usually has sulphur in it. This pollutes the air when it is burned.

Bituminous coal

Bituminous coal is black. It is found deeper under the ground

than lignite. Bituminous coal has fewer impurities than lignite. This means that bituminous coal burns at a higher temperature and causes less **pollution** than lignite. There is more bituminous coal than any other kind.

Anthracite
Anthracite is found even deeper down under the ground than bituminous coal. It is the best coal. It is black and shiny. Sometimes it is used for jewellery.

Left: Lignite is found near the surface, so it is easier to mine.

Middle: Bituminous coal is darker in colour and is found further under ground.

Right: Anthracite is the blackest coal of all. It is found in thin layers deep beneath the surface.

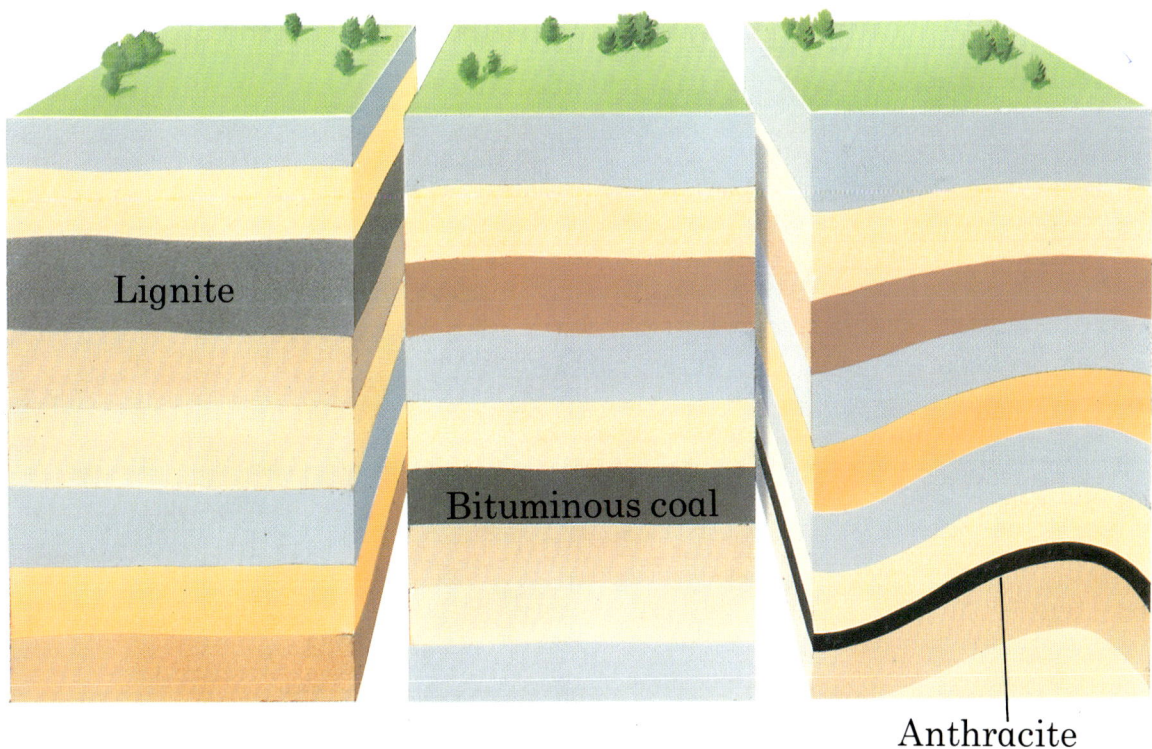

Lignite

Bituminous coal

Anthracite

Mining Coal

Coal facts

● Coal and oil contain a great deal of carbon. This means that they burn well.
● Today, electric trains and conveyor belts bring coal up to the surface from the deep mine shafts. In the past the coal was carried by men, women and children. Sometimes the coal was put into carts and hauled up by dogs, ponies and goats.

Sometimes layers of coal may be uncovered by earthquakes, by the wind and rain or by waves around coasts. This was probably how people first discovered coal. The earliest coal-mines were dug by people who followed the seam of coal they had discovered into the ground. The deeper they dug the more danger there was of the sides caving in on them. Today we use two different methods of mining coal. One is called deep-shaft mining. This involves digging long shafts and tunnels deep into the ground. The tunnels are propped up to prevent them collapsing.

This is an opencast mine in Germany. The lignite coal that is being dug up is very close to the surface. ▶

Opencast mining

In opencast mining the earth is scraped away to uncover the coal beneath. Huge machines are used to do this. Opencast mining is cheaper than deep-shaft mining but it can do great damage to the landscape.

The miners in deep-shaft mines use machines to help them drill. Trains and elevators are then used to carry the coal up to the surface where it is stored in huge stock piles. ▼

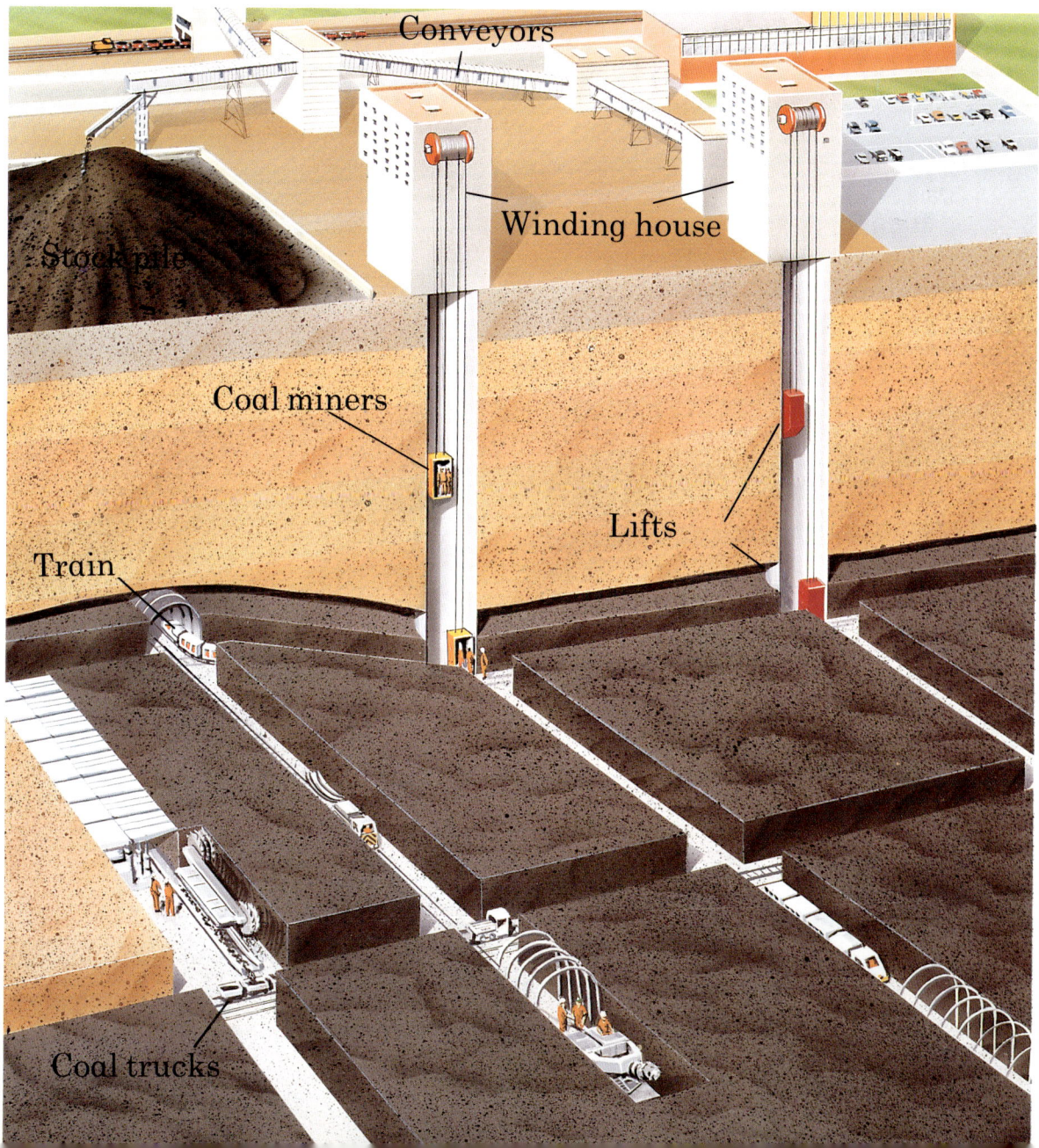

Conveyors

Winding house

Stockpile

Coal miners

Lifts

Train

Coal trucks

Putting Coal to Work

Steam-engines use the heat of burning coal to turn water into steam. Early steam-engines used the steam to move **pistons** up and down to run machines. Later, steam-engines were used to turn turbines. Turbines are used to generate electricity.

Burning coal produces more heat than burning wood. The heat coal gives can be used to make

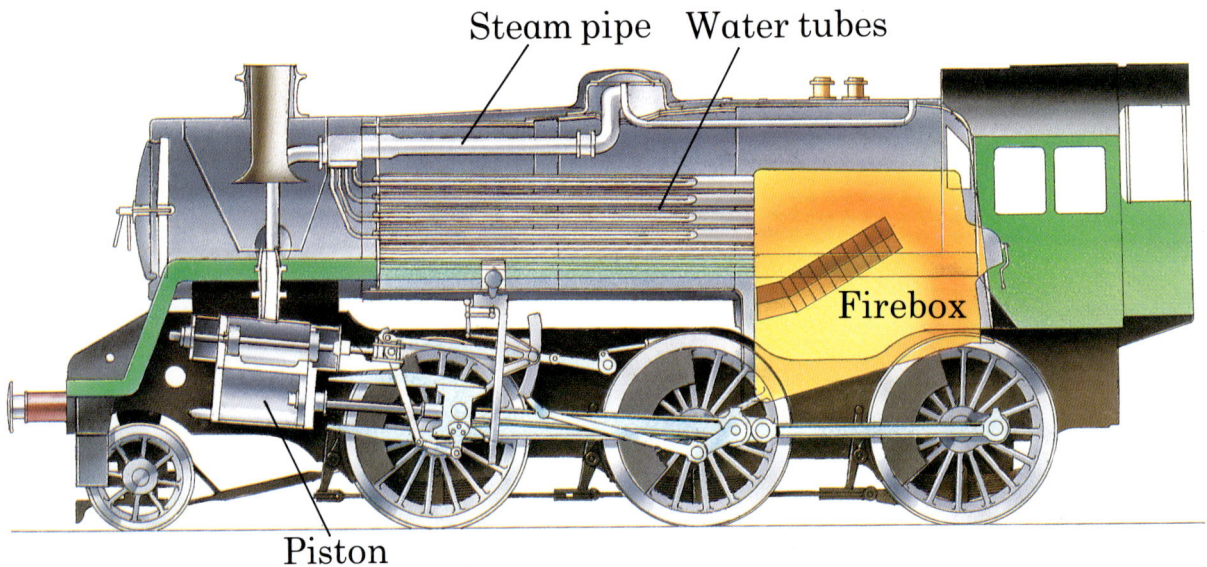

Steam pipe   Water tubes

Firebox

Piston

▲ This steam-engine is run by steam power. Coal is burned in the firebox. This heats water to make steam. The steam then moves the pistons, and the pistons make the wheels go round.

stronger and better metals, such as steel. These metals can then be used to make strong machines and tools.

Coke
Charcoal is sometimes called the super-fuel version of wood. The

super fuel version of coal is called coke. Coke is made by heating coal in special ovens that keep out air. This removes moisture and impurities from the coal. A gas is given off when this is done. It can be used as a fuel. What is left of the coal is called coke. Coke burns longer and gives more heat than coal. It also causes less pollution.

▲ Inside a coal-fired power station. A large boiler turns water into steam. The steam travels through large metal pipes to the turbine. The steam spins the turbine blades and electricity is generated.

◄ A modern coking oven where coal is made into coke. The coke comes out red hot and must be allowed to cool before it can be used.

The Fuel Revolution

A **textile** mill where ▶ cloth was made over a hundred years ago. A steam-engine is used to turn the long overhead shafts. The leather belts above then turn the **looms**.

This traction engine uses steam power to help the farmer thresh the crops. ▼

Coal was the fuel that made the Industrial Revolution possible. Unlike water and wind, coal could be moved easily from one place to another. Reliable stocks of coal provided a constant supply of fuel. Once it is mined coal is easy to use. The first coal-powered steam-engines were used for stationary, or non-moving, tasks. These engines replaced the muscle power of human and animal workers. Early steam-engines were used to

The earliest steam-engines were used to pump water out of coal-mines. Later they were used to run other machines. ▼

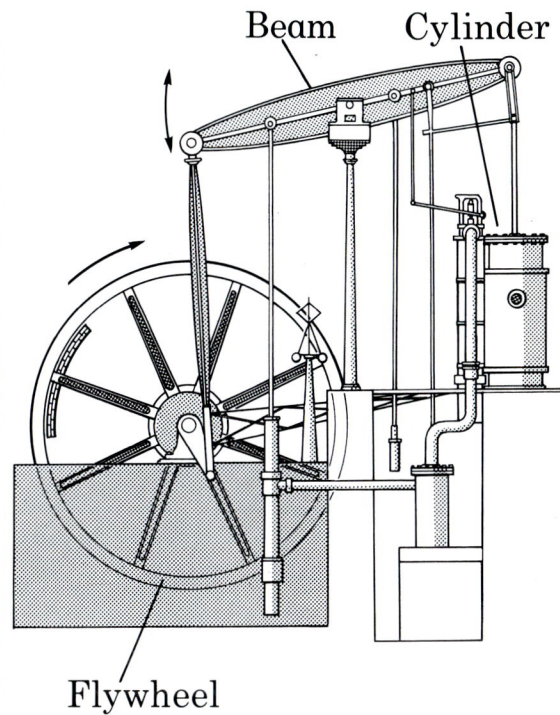

Beam   Cylinder

Flywheel

help pump water, weave fabric and carve wood, as well as many other things.

In 1829 George Stephenson used steam power to move his famous locomotive, the Rocket. He showed that railways could carry people and objects further and faster than the horse and cart. Farmers also made use of the new steam-engines. Traction engines (later called tractors) were invented to help farmers plough fields and **thresh** grain.

A steam train in China, where coal is still used to operate some trains. ▼

Black Gold

Petroleum oil provides a third of the energy we use. It is refined into fuel oil, petrol, diesel and kerosene, all of which can be used as fuels. ▼

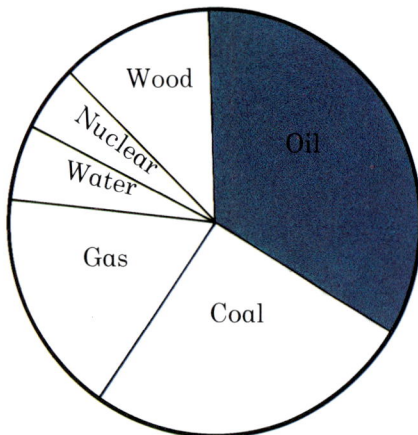

Like coal, oil is a fossil fuel. It can be found many hundreds of metres under the ground or under the bottom of the sea. ▶

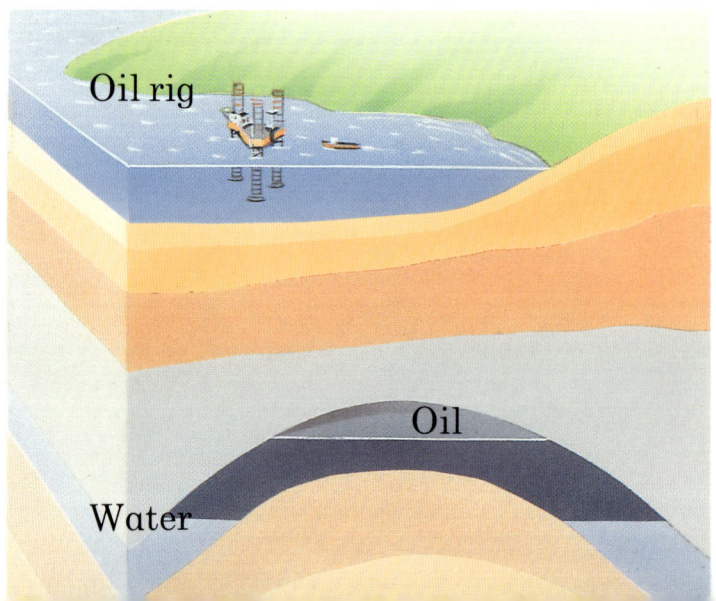

CHAPTER SEVEN

PETROLEUM OIL

Just as coal is sometimes called 'black diamonds', liquid petroleum oil is known as 'black gold'. This shows how important petroleum oil is in the world today. It is used for many things. It is used to grease things such as hinges to make them work more smoothly. It is an ingredient in many kinds of plastics, paints, polishes, pesticides and cosmetics. More importantly, petroleum oil is used as a fuel. About one-third of the energy we use comes from petroleum oil.

In this oil refinery crude oil is processed into many
◄ different products.

Types of oil

There are many different kinds of oil. Some, such as cod liver oil, come from animals. Others, such as sunflower oil, come from plants. Mineral oils, such as petroleum, are mined from the earth. Petroleum oil when it first comes out of the ground is called crude oil. Crude oil can be brown, yellow or green.

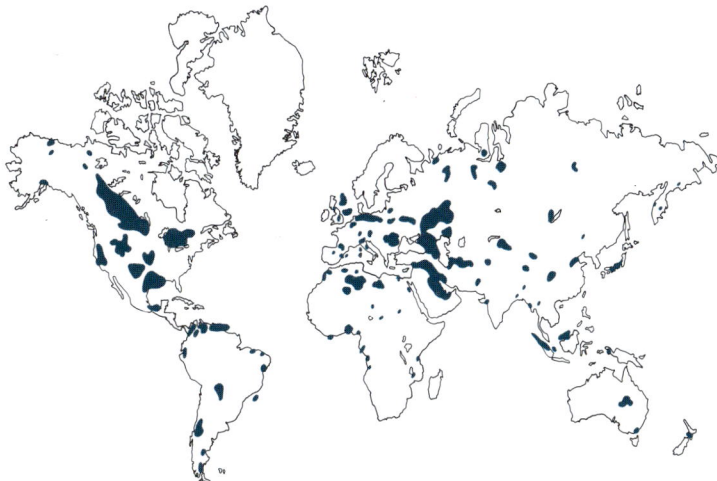

Oil facts

● Usually about three-quarters of oil is carbon.
● In Shaanxi Province, China, the oil is so thick it can be cut into blocks like butter. Small fires are burned under the storage tanks to keep the oil liquid enough to flow.

Petroleum oil is found in many places. Four countries – Saudi Arabia, Kuwait, Iran and the United Arab Emirates hold half of the world's
◄ known oil.

Digging Deep

These workers are drilling for oil in Saudi Arabia. ▶

More oil facts

● The very first oil well was actually drilled in the 1840s. Someone in Ohio, USA, was drilling for salt but found oil instead. Not knowing how valuable his find was the digger thought his well was a failure.

● The world's largest known oil field is the Ghawar Field in Saudi Arabia. It measures 240 kilometres by 35 kilometres

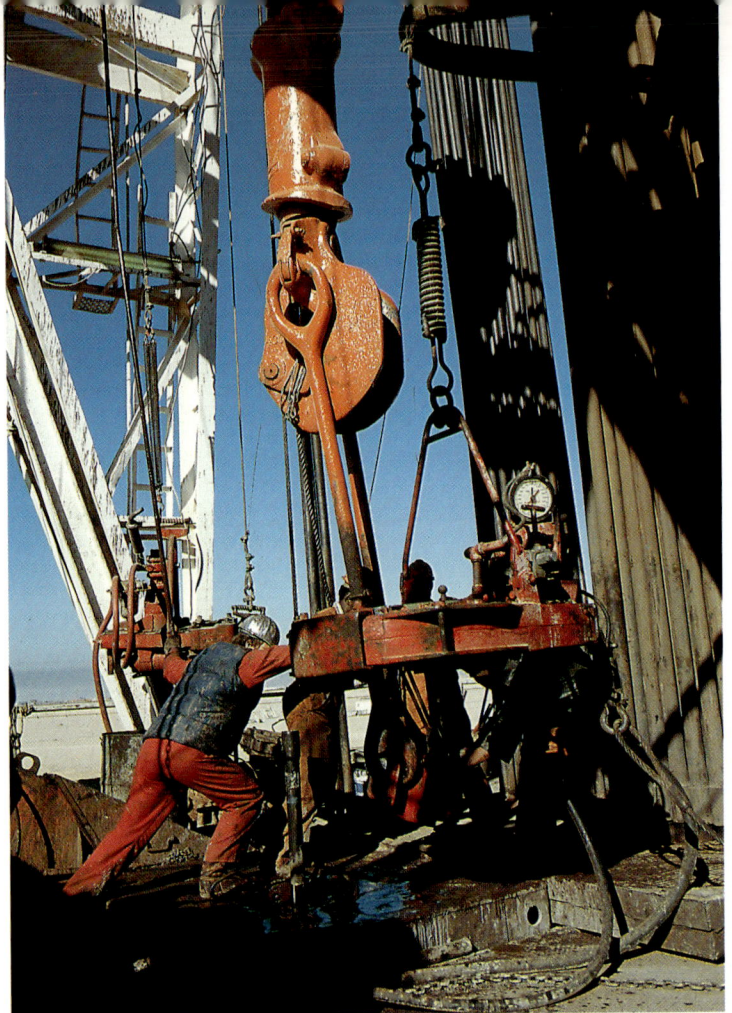

Because oil is a liquid it cannot just be dug up in the same way coal can. Most crude oil is trapped deep under the ground. Sometimes it leaks up to form puddles on the ground. This was how people first found out about oil. We drill wells now to pump this liquid fuel from the ground. The first successful oil well was drilled in 1859 in Titusville, Pennsylvania, USA. Since then, oil wells have been drilled all over the world.

Searching for oil

It is very difficult to tell where there might be oil just by looking at the ground. Oil might be found under farms, deserts, **tundra** or even under the bottom of the ocean. Early searchers for oil had to guess where it might be. If they were wrong they would drill an expensive well and find nothing but rocks. Today we have machines that can tell us what is under the ground before we start to drill.

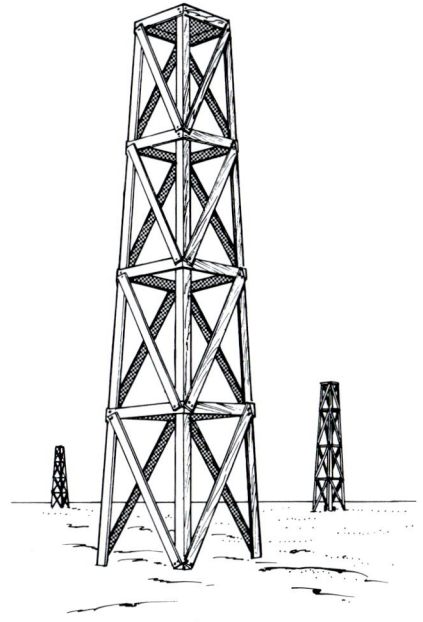

▲ The sturdy steel towers that hold the drilling gear above land are called derricks. They have to be very tall to support the long drills.

This derrick is used for drilling oil in Alaska. Special drills must be used to break through the ◀ frozen ground.

Digging deep

● Oil wells have to reach the oil far below the surface. Some are as much as 2 kilometres deep.
● Some deep-sea oil platforms are almost as big as the biggest building on Earth.

39

Oil Wells and Refineries

A drill bit with sharp teeth to grind through rocks. Drill bits are used to cut through to the oil deep under the ground. ▼

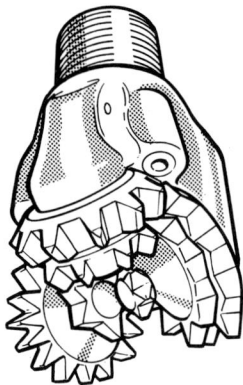

Once people know that there is oil under the ground a derrick, or drilling rig, is set up. The derrick is a large steel structure that holds the drill, pipes and other equipment. After the oil has been reached the derrick is taken down. Next, the oil has to be brought out. Sometimes the oil will gush out on its own. Other times, pumps have to be used to bring it to the surface. If the oil is very deep down sometimes gas has to be pumped into the well to force the oil up to the surface.

Oil refining

Crude oil can be used straight from the ground for some things. For most purposes, however, the

This oil production platform floats on the ocean's surface. Several wells have been drilled on the ocean floor. ▶

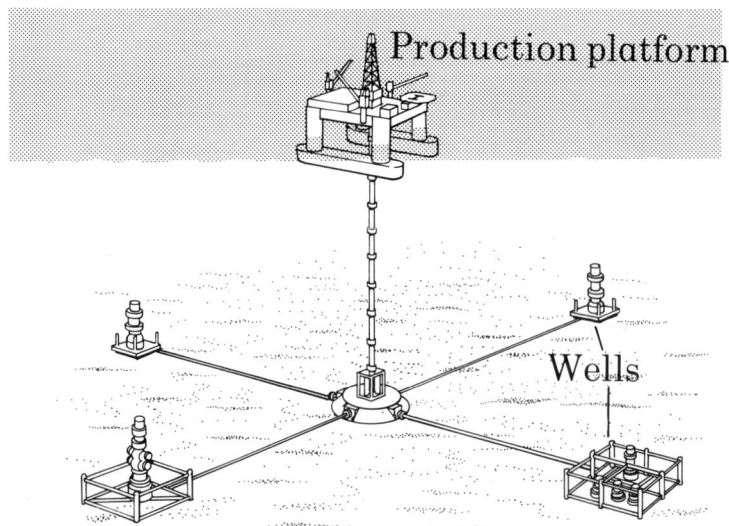

Production platform

Wells

oil must be processed and refined. Most petroleum oil is refined into other forms, such as petrol for cars, heating oil, kerosene, diesel oil for trucks and buses and so on. There are hundreds of uses for this valuable 'black gold'.

▲ Deep-sea oil platforms can be huge. Some are as tall as the Eiffel Tower in Paris, France. The platforms are often moved hundreds of kilometres from the place where they were built to the place where they will work.

This pipeline carries oil across Alaska, USA, from wells inland to the sea. From there the oil will be carried around the world ◄ in giant oil tankers.

41

Putting Oil to Work

A scarce resource?

Our supplies of oil are running out. This is because we use so much of it for so many things. No one is sure when we will actually run out of oil. People are searching for new oil supplies and ways to get more oil from old wells. Even so, the oil will not last for ever.

Fairly simple engines, such as those in some lawnmowers, can run on petroleum oil. ▶

Just as coal is a better fuel than wood, so oil is a better fuel than coal. Oil burns better than coal, so not so much needs to be used. Oil also burns more cleanly than coal so it does not cause so much pollution. Oil fires can be turned on and off quickly and easily. Coal fires can't very easily be put out and started again. Oil can be used as a fuel for almost everything that coal can.

Fuel oil

Oil can be put to work for us in many ways. It can be burned in power stations to provide electricity. The oil is burned in a boiler, where it heats water. When the water is turned into steam it is sent along pipes to the turbines. The turbines are then

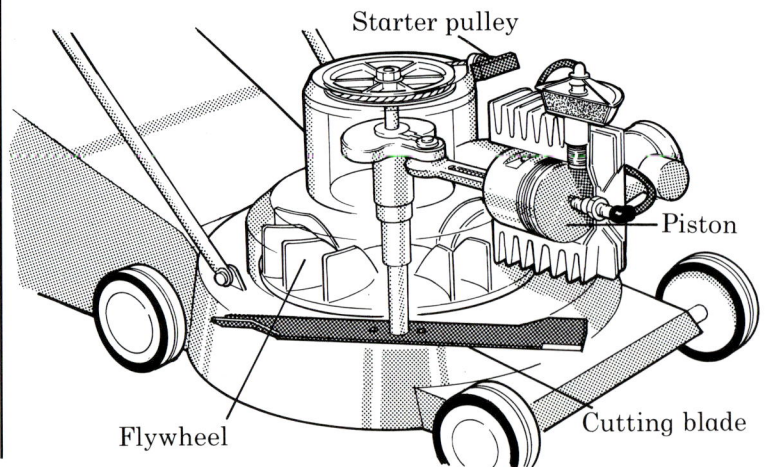

Starter pulley

Piston

Flywheel

Cutting blade

42

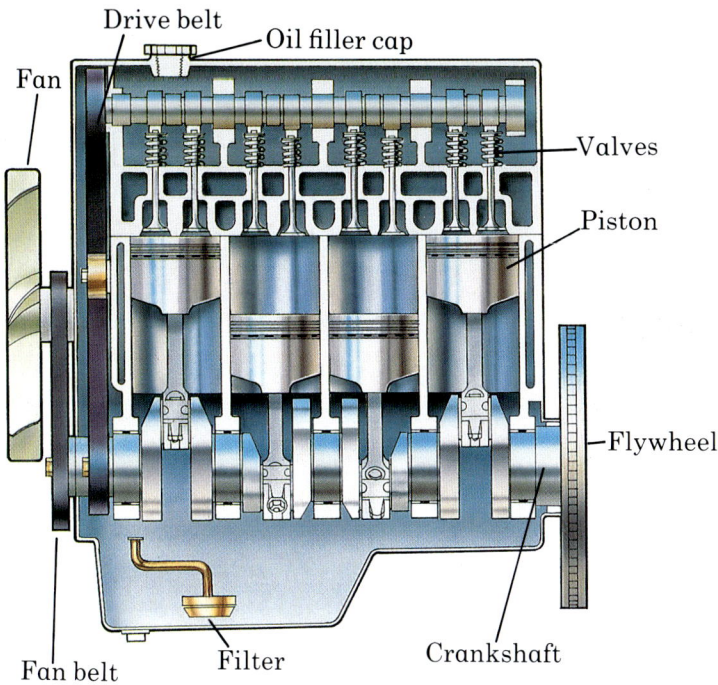

Drive belt — Oil filler cap
Fan
Valves
Piston
Flywheel
Fan belt — Filter — Crankshaft

◄ This picture shows what the inside of a car engine looks like.

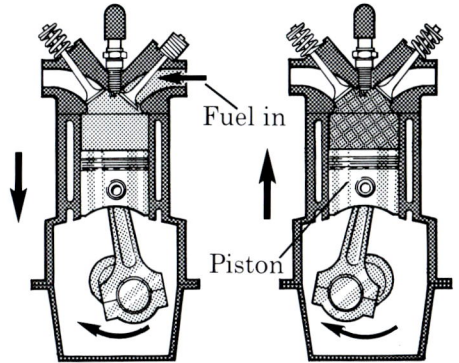

Fuel in
Piston

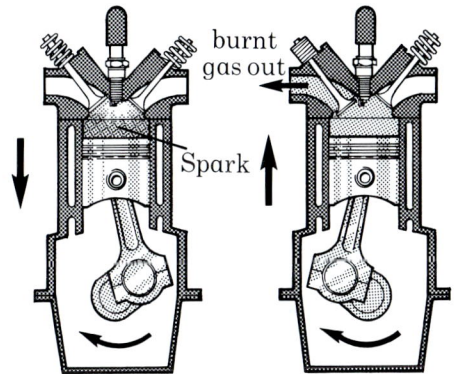

burnt gas out
Spark

made to spin, generating electricity.

Oil can also be used in engines. Here the energy of the oil is used to make pistons move up and down. The movement of the pistons is then made to do work. Another kind of oil is used in jet engines. Here it is mixed with air before it is burned. The burning gases then spin the turbines.

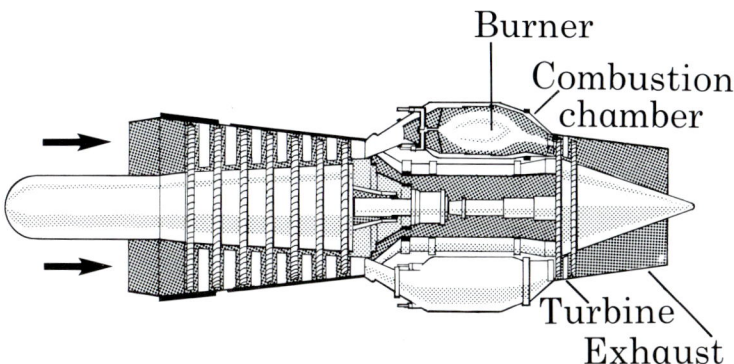

Burner
Combustion chamber
Turbine
Exhaust

▲ In a car engine, first, the piston moves down. This sucks in air and fuel. Then it moves back up, squeezing the mixture into a smaller space. A spark ignites the mixture, forcing the piston back down. Lastly, the burnt gases are released and it all starts again.

◄ Jet engines burn a mixture of fuel and air.

43

The History of Gas

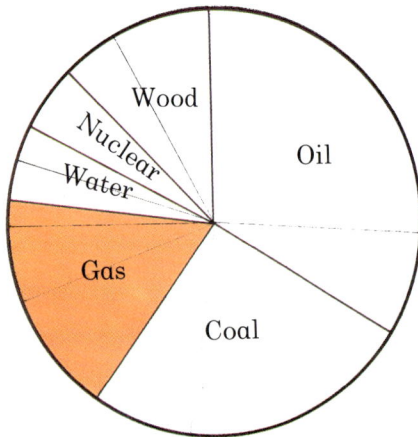

▲ Gas is the third most important fossil fuel.

Gas is sometimes found with oil. Usually it is just burned off. ▶

CHAPTER EIGHT

GAS

It is only in the last fifty years or so that natural gas has become a valued fuel. **Prospectors** looking for coal or oil would be unhappy if they found gas instead. Today, natural gas is an important fuel. It provides about one-fifth of our energy needs.

Artificial and natural gas

The first street lights were fuelled by **artificial** gas from coal. This gas was produced when coal was turned into coke. It was the first gas to be used as a fuel. Natural

Coal

Steam and oxygen

Ash

Gas

Treatment plant

Gas

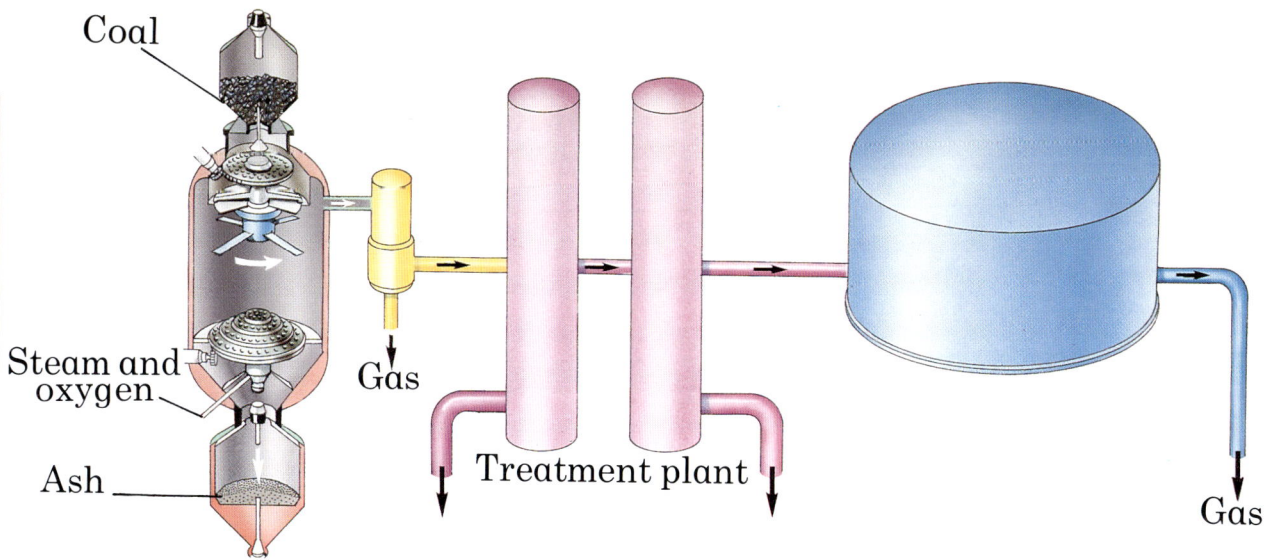

gas is usually found in rock under the ground. These rocks have millions of tiny holes. They act like sponges and soak up the gas as it is formed. Above this rock there are layers of heavier rock that trap the gas underground and stop it from leaking out to the surface.

Natural gas is really a mixture of different gases. Almost all of these gases are made from carbon and hydrogen.

▲ In order to produce gas of high quality from coal. The coal is first burned keeping most of the air out. The gas is then cleaned up.

Major gas fields are shown here. Gas is found in fewer places than coal ◄ or oil.

45

Putting Gas to Work

These huge tanks at Mab Ta Pud, Thailand, hold natural gas. ▶

Did you know?

● Natural gas has no smell. Its smell has been added for safety. If you smell gas, tell an adult at once.

● After gas is taken from the ground it is cleaned up. It is then pumped into giant storage tanks. Large pipelines carry the gas great distances from the tanks to places around the country. Giant engines similar to jet engines push the gas through the pipelines. Smaller pipes then carry it to individual users.

People have known about natural gas for a long time. In 1272, the traveller Marco Polo reported seeing natural gas burning at Baku in what is now the Soviet Union. We now know how to use natural gas safely. It is commonly used in the home for heating and cooking. It is also used for many industrial purposes.

Advantages of gas

Gas has many advantages over other fuels. It can be made to burn hotter than coal or oil. It is also very convenient to use. It can be lit and put out again easily. It has

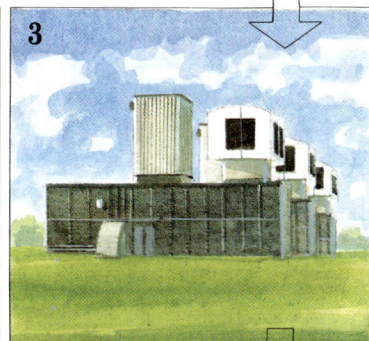

another advantage. When it is very, very cold natural gas turns into a liquid. This liquid is called liquid petroleum gas or LPG. It can be moved from place to place in special bottles. In areas that do not have gas pipelines many people use LPG for heating and cooking.

▲ Gas is pumped from production platforms sometimes out at sea (1) to processing plants on shore (2). It is then sent to a **compressor station** (3) and then to storage tanks (4). The gas company (5) makes sure that the gas is supplied to the people who need it. Gas meters in people's homes (6) record how much gas is used. It may be used to fuel a cooker (7).

Power from Atoms

Nuclear power provides less of our energy than any other source. It provides less energy than wood or water. ▼

In atomic fission energy is released when atoms split apart. In atomic fusion energy is released when atoms are joined together.
▶

CHAPTER NINE
NUCLEAR POWER

Atomic energy is energy that is released from atoms. It is the most powerful source of energy we have. It is the energy that powers the sun.

Fission and fusion

There are two ways in which atoms can give off energy. Atoms give off energy when they are split into smaller atoms and bits of atoms. This is called fission. Some substances break down into smaller atoms naturally.

Fission

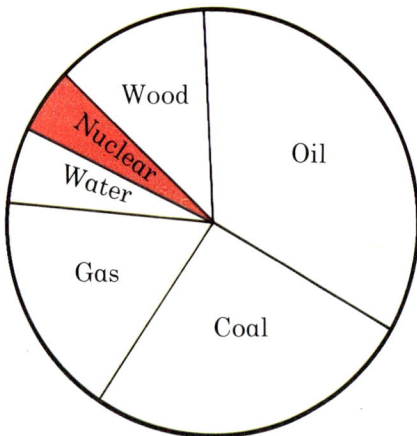

Atoms splitting

Atoms joining

Fusion

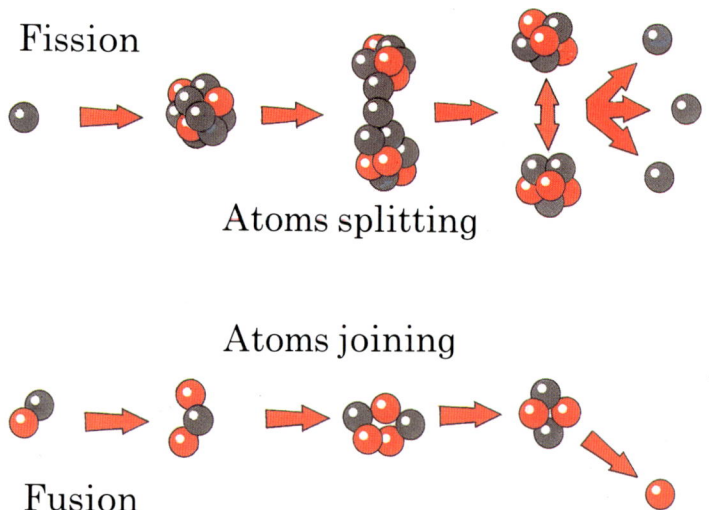

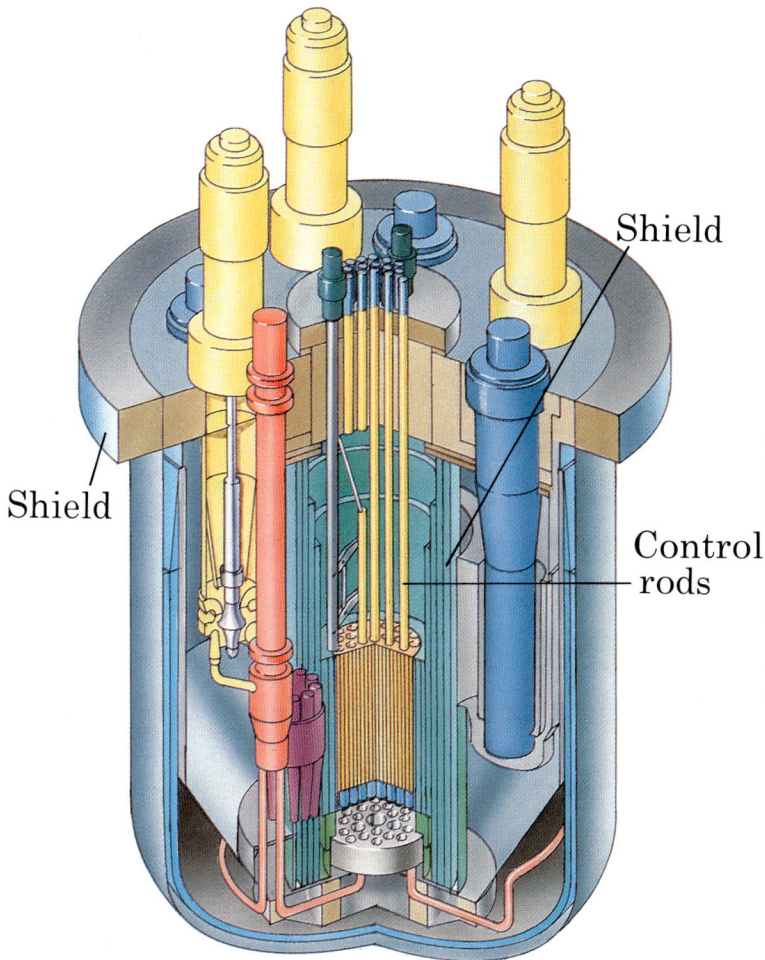

Shield

Shield

Control rods

◄ Nuclear **reactors** are very complicated. They have many safety devices to protect the people who work with them.

▲ The nuclear reactions that go on in the sun provide us with heat and light here on Earth.

Nuclear facts

Atoms can be split by making neutrons crash into them at very high speeds. Neutrons are bits of atoms.

Substances that do this are said to be radioactive.

Two atoms can also be made to join together to form a bigger atom. When this happens a great deal of energy is released. This process is called fusion. It is atomic fusion that produced the energy of the sun and provides the Earth with light and heat. People have been trying to find a way to make the energy of fusion available for use.

49

Nuclear Energy

An accident at the ▶ Chernobyl nuclear power station in the Soviet Union affected people in many countries. Harmful radioactive substances were released into the air and carried for thousands of kilometres by the wind.

When nuclear energy was first discovered some people thought that it would solve all our energy problems. They said that it would produce all the power we would ever need. Unfortunately, it turned out to be more expensive to produce nuclear power than had been thought.

Nuclear power stations make electricity in much the same way as those using fossil fuels. Both types use heat energy to make steam, which then turns the turbines that make the electricity.

Nuclear problems

Nuclear power stations need only a small amount of fuel but the

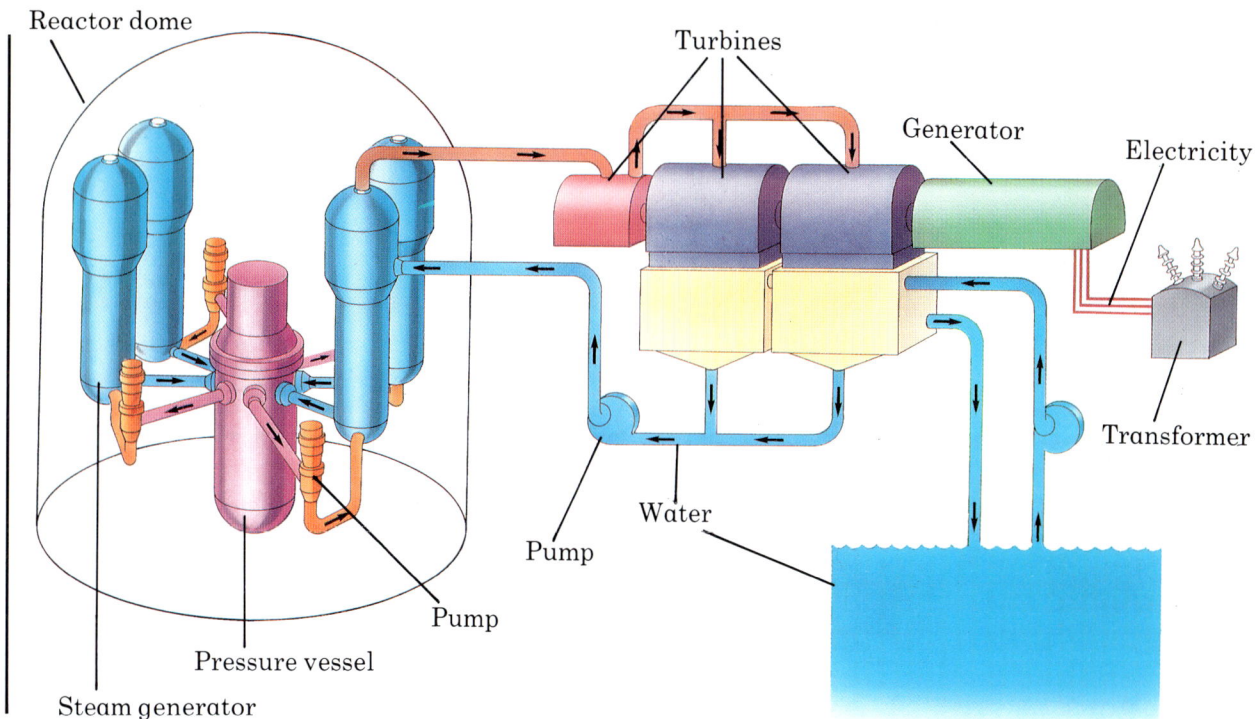

Reactor dome

Turbines

Generator

Electricity

Transformer

Pump

Water

Pump

Pressure vessel

Steam generator

▲ This diagram shows how a nuclear power plant produces steam to make electricity.

A nuclear power station in France. Power stations like this need a lot of ◄ water for cooling.

costs of building them can be high. This can mean that the electricity they produce is very expensive. Nuclear energy can also be dangerous. If radioactive substances get into the air or water they can poison whole areas for many years.

Making Electricity

Electricity is so much a part of our lives that we tend to take it for granted. How many things can you think of that use electricity? ▶

CHAPTER TEN
ELECTRICITY

People still do not understand fully what electricity actually is. This, of course, has not stopped us from using it.

Generating electricity
Today most electricity is made in power stations. As described earlier, these can produce electricity using a number of sources of energy. They can use water, fossil fuels or nuclear energy.

Hydroelectric power stations

◄ Lightning is a form of electricity called static electricity that occurs naturally. The electric charge builds up on the surface of something that does not allow electricity to pass through it.

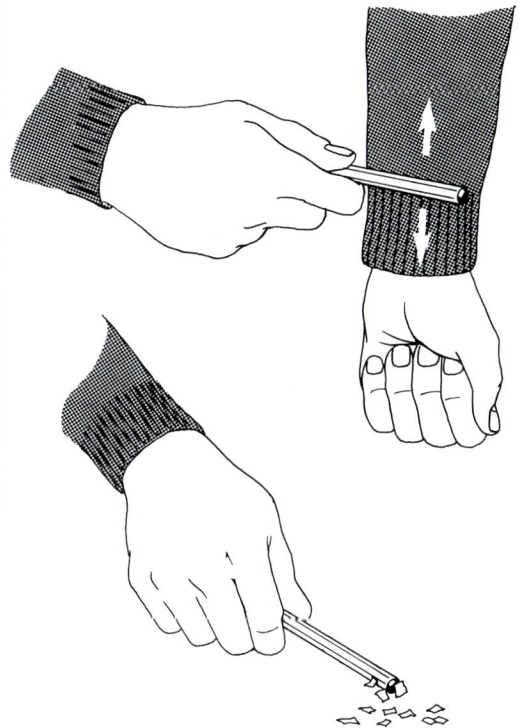

use the force of flowing water to spin the turbines that make the electricity. Fossil fuel and nuclear power stations first produce heat energy. This is used to turn water into steam. The steam is then used to spin their turbines. Power stations that use heat to make electricity are called **thermal** power stations. Most of the electricity we use is made in this way.

▲ You can make static electricity by rubbing a glass rod on a woollen jumper. Hold the rod over some bits of paper and see what happens.

Working For Us

When electricity is made, a lot of energy is lost in the form of heat. Some energy is also lost in actually getting the electricity to flow along the wires that carry it to where it is needed. Because of this power stations need to be reasonably close to the people who need the electricity.

Electricity grids

The wires that carry electricity to homes and factories stretch high above the ground or are

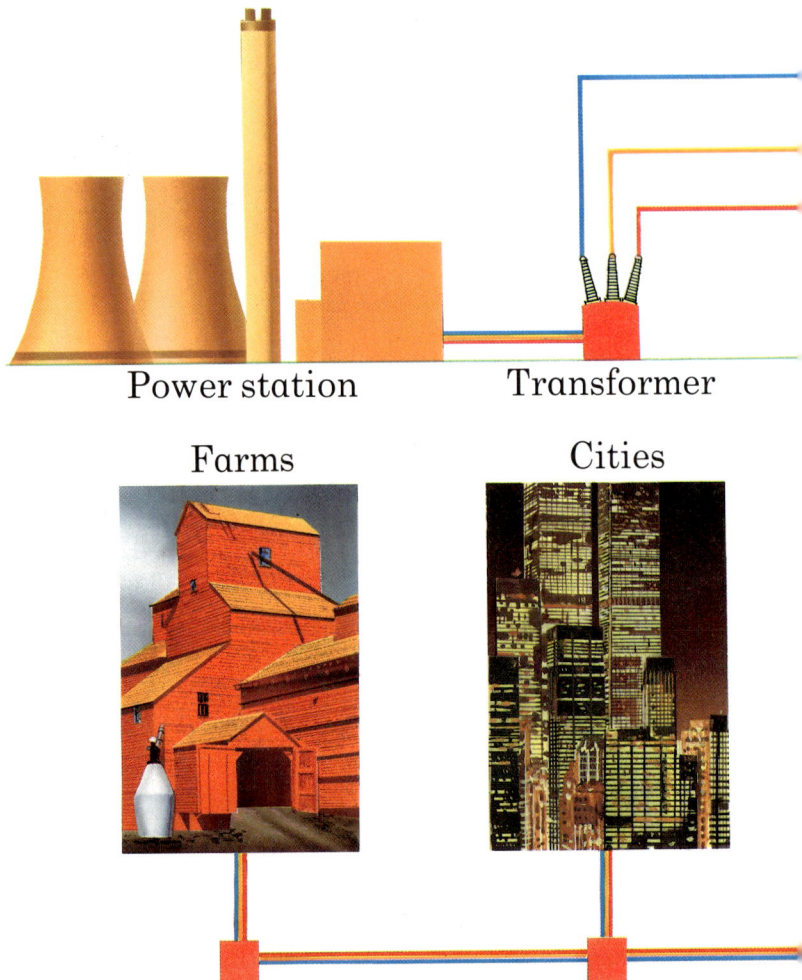

Power stations

● The world's largest coal-fired power station is in Ekibastuz, Kazakhstan, USSR.
● The world's most powerful electricity generating station is the Grand Coulee Dam, Washington, USA.

When electricity leaves a power station it is far too powerful and dangerous for most uses. **Transformers** and substations bring it down to the level of power needed. ▶

Power station

Transformer

Farms

Cities

buried underneath it. This keeps people safe from the dangerous electricity. Power stations and the wires that connect them to users of electricity are called an electricity grid.

Batteries

Batteries make electricity from chemical energy. They only produce fairly small amounts of electricity. They don't last very long, either. This makes them expensive to use.

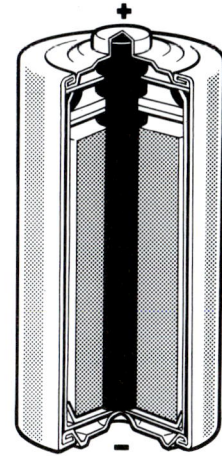

▲ Batteries are convenient sources of electricity for certain uses. They can be used in torches, radios, toys and many other things that it might not be convenient to plug into the main electrical supply.

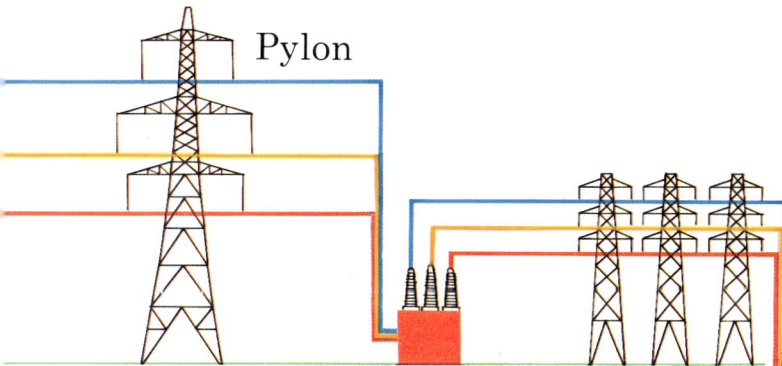

Pylon

Hospitals

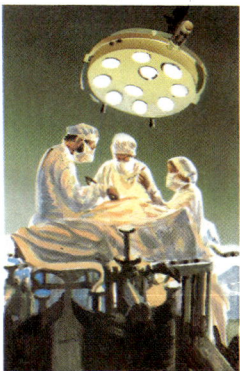

Industry

Power failure

The biggest power failure ever happened on the night of 9 November 1965. Seven states of the USA and part of Canada were without electricity. About 30 million people were in darkness.

Fuels of the Future

CHAPTER ELEVEN

THE FUTURE

Every year there are more and more people using more and more energy. We need to find new sources of energy before the ones we have run out. Our planet has only a limited amount of coal, oil and gas for use as fuels.

Making better use of resources

People are looking for better ways to make use of the energy that we have now. Power stations turn less than half of the energy from the fossil fuels they use into

Oil spills are a waste of precious fuel. They also do terrible damage to the environment. Here efforts are being made to keep oil from reaching the coast of Alaska, USA. Thousands of birds and other animals can be killed by oil spills. ▶

Number of years fossil fuels may last

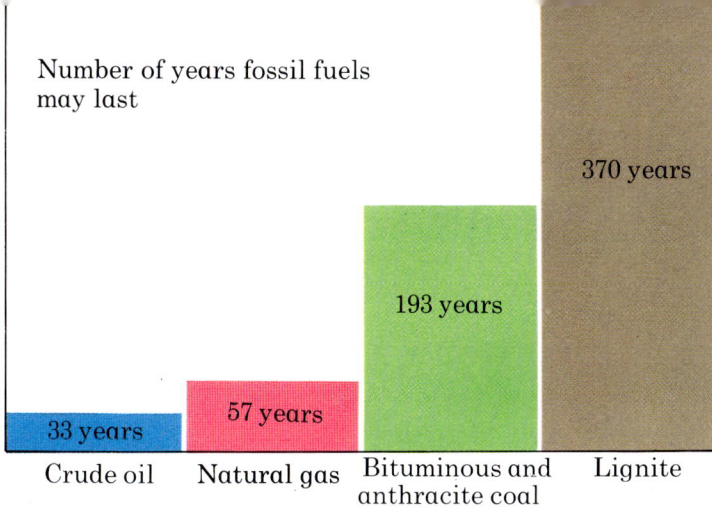

- 33 years — Crude oil
- 57 years — Natural gas
- 193 years — Bituminous and anthracite coal
- 370 years — Lignite

Our supplies of fossil fuels are running out. Some people think that we will have used up all the oil we have in fifty years or less. Our supplies of coal will probably last for several hundred years. We still need to look for new sources of energy, however, because coal cannot supply all our ◄ needs.

electricity. The rest of it is wasted. This lost energy could perhaps be used to heat homes and factories.

People are searching for new sources of fossil fuels. New methods of mining coal are being developed. Deep-sea oil rigs are also being used. Ways of getting as much as possible from the coal and oil fields we know about are being found too.

In Copenhagen, Denmark, waste heat from this power station is used to heat homes and factories. ▼

Alternative Energy Sources

This is a solar power station that makes electricity from the energy of the sun. ▶

People are always looking for new sources of energy that are clean, safe and renewable. We have seen how scientists are looking at new ways of using wind and water power.

Solar power

The energy of sunlight, called **solar** power, is used in several ways. One way is to collect it in solar cells. These make electricity from sunlight. Solar cells can power radios and even small cars. Solar furnaces use giant mirrors to focus the sun's rays on a boiler. Steam from the boiler is used to

A power station in Iceland that uses heat from the inside of the Earth to ◄ produce electricity.

make electricity. Solar panels collect heat energy from the sun.

Earth power

Some people are trying to find ways to use heat from inside the Earth. Natural hot water and steam from deep under the ground provide energy.

▲ The Castle Geyser in Yellowstone National Park, USA, shoots streams of naturally heated water high into the air.

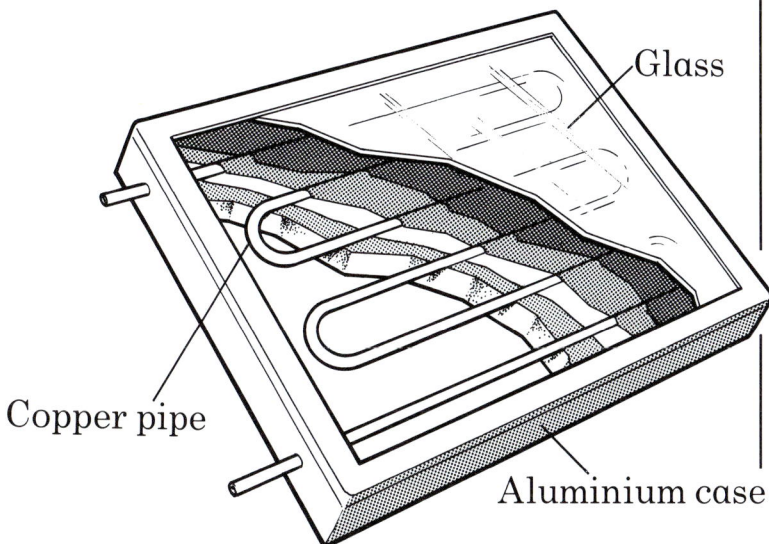

Glass

Copper pipe

Aluminium case

◄ A diagram of a solar panel. It collects heat from the sun and uses it to heat water.

59

Glossary

Artificial: something made by people; the opposite of natural.

Atomic: to do with atoms.

Blast furnace: a very hot furnace used for making iron and steel.

Canal: an artificial waterway dug to join together different rivers or seas.

Chemical: to do with chemistry. Chemistry is the study of substances, what they are made of, and how they react with each other.

Compressor: something that squeezes things together.

Energy: the power or the ability to do work.

Estuary: the wide mouth of a river where it meets the sea.

Experiment: a test carried out to discover if something will happen.

Fossil: the remains of something that lived millions of years ago and has been preserved in rock.

Generator: a machine for changing mechanical energy into electrical energy.

Hero: a Greek scientist and inventor who lived around 2000 years ago.

Impurity: a substance mixed in small amounts with another substance.

Industrial Revolution: a period of history from about 1740 to 1850 when factories were first built and many inventions, such as the steam-engine, appeared.

Loom: a machine for weaving thread into cloth.

Mechanical: to do with machines.

Nuclear: to do with a part of an atom called the nucleus.

Piston: a circular piece of metal that moves up and down inside a cylinder to produce mechanical energy.

Plantation: plants of the same kind that are grown together and looked after by people.

Pollution: something that spoils or poisons our surroundings.

Prospector: someone who explores an area looking for valuable things such as oil or gold.

Reactor: the part of a nuclear power station where atoms are split. This gives a great deal of energy.

Resource: something that can be put to good use, such as a supply of energy or materials for building.

Robot: a machine that can be instructed to do certain jobs.

Solar: to do with the sun.

Textile: any kind of cloth.

Thermal: to do with heat.

Thresh: to separate the grains of a cereal from the husks and the straw.

Transformer: something for changing an electrical current.

Transportation: the means of moving people and things from one place to another. Buses and trucks are forms of transportation.

Tundra: the vast nearly flat lands of the north where no trees grow. Tundra is found in the northern areas of Canada and the USSR.

Turbine: a motor in which blades are made to spin, usually by steam.

Index

A number in **bold** shows the entry is illustrated on that page. The same page often has writing about the entry too.